# Be Bold, Walk Tall

*by*
*Lester Sumrall*

# Be Bold, Walk Tall

*by*
*Lester Sumrall*

**Harrison House, Inc.**
Tulsa, Oklahoma

Unless otherwise indicated, all Scripture quotations are taken from the *King James Version* of the Bible.

*Be Bold, Walk Tall*
ISBN 0-89274-776-5
Copyright © 1995 by Lester Sumrall
Evangelistic Association, Inc.
South Bend, Indiana 46624

Published by Harrison House, Inc.
P.O. Box 35035
Tulsa, OK 74153

# Contents

# 1
# A Slave Who Was Bold and Walked Tall

# 1
# A Slave Who Was Bold and Walked Tall

Write on your doors the saying wise and old,

"Be bold! be bold!" and everywhere, "Be bold!;

Be not too bold!" Yet better the excess than the defect; better the more than less.[1]

— Henry Wadsworth Longfellow

If you want to be bold and walk tall in God, it will require complete obedience.

If you want to walk tall in God — be like Caleb of the Israelites.

He could say with confidence, "I entirely followed the Lord my God when no one but Joshua was with me. The others refused to

---

[1]Seldes, George, compiler, *Great Quotations*, "Morituri Salutamus," (New York: Pocket Books, 1960, 1969), pp. 89,90.

take the land God promised us, but I followed God."

**And Moses sware on that day, saying, Surely the land whereon thy feet have trodden shall be thine inheritance, and thy children's for ever, because thou hast wholly followed the Lord my God.**

**Joshua 14:9**

Look at the result of Caleb's obedience: Everywhere his feet trod was given to him, not just for his own inheritance, but to go to his children's children in perpetuity. (Deut. 1:36.)

What are *your* children going to receive in this life? If you wholly follow the Lord your God, then your seed can possess everything that God has for you and them.

I have always felt sorry for Christians who do not pass on their heritage of godliness to their children. Many do not bother to send, much less take, their children to church activities. When those children are older, they will not want church at all.

Then the parents will scream, "Oh, God! Save my children!" And they will blame the church for what is happening.

We have lost so many children from our churches, because their parents — who *were* Christians — did not see that they attended Sunday school and youth activities. God promised to bless our children, but we have to do our part by keeping them in church where they can hear His Word and learn to fellowship with the saints.

Notice something else about Caleb:

He knew God had kept him alive for a purpose. He was determined to fulfill his destiny in God, although he was eighty-five years old before he could begin to possess his promised inheritance.

> **And now, behold, the Lord hath kept me alive, as he said, these forty and five years, even since the Lord spake this word unto Moses, while the children of Israel wandered in the wilderness: and now, lo, I am this day fourscore and five years old.**
> **Joshua 14:10**

Look at Caleb's boldness even in his old age. When the Israelites finally were ready to go into the Promised Land, Caleb reminded them that God had kept him alive since the first time he spied out the land.

He was bold to excess, but that was better than being cowardly and not having the courage to go into the land at all. Also, being bold sometimes means having to wait on other people to get ready to move.

It would have been nice if God had simply built Caleb and Joshua a little camp on the edge of the Promised Land and let them stay there until the next-generation Israelites got ready to move.

But, then, who would have been an example for them?

Who would have led them when Moses and Aaron passed on?

The Israelites were able to see a contrast in Joshua and Caleb between boldness and its reward and the devastation brought by the devil because of fear running in God's people. Sometimes we have to witness the destruction that doubt, unbelief, fear, and sin bring before we develop the boldness to be obedient.

But God is faithful, and He kept Caleb alive in order for him to enter the land as He had promised. God always is faithful to His promises. The Lord will keep you alive and provide special blessings, as long as you walk in faith, obedience, and boldness.

## The Bold Receive From God

I have met dozens of people around the world, who said to me, "I *thought* one day you would come here to preach! God has kept me alive to see you and to hear these truths you teach. I'm old, but I have received the Holy Spirit, and God has kept me alive for this very day!"

That always makes me think of what many Christians desire more than anything — to be alive when Jesus returns. There may be millions of Christians who will live beyond their age limits in the natural, because God has said to them, "Yes, I will grant that you can be alive when I come back."

To my mind, that would be the greatest gift a human being could ever receive! The most wonderful thing that could happen to us as Christians in this life would be to be alive when Jesus comes back and to go up to meet Him in the air.

I can tell you from personal experience that faithfulness to God is a great thing.

Caleb said, "God has kept me alive these forty and five years."

That means he spent the first forty years of his life in Egypt, forty years wandering the desert, and another five years serving Joshua and helping the Israelites gain the Promised Land.

He trailed Joshua around, chasing the enemy out of the land, so his people could possess it. He must have been a remarkable man of faith at eighty-five years old.

After all, he had bones just as we have bones.

He had hair just as we have hair.

He had teeth just as we have teeth.

Yet the Bible says his strength was as that of a man of forty. He was as strong as the day Moses first sent him to spy out the land of Canaan with Joshua and ten other Israelites.

He was as human as you or me, yet he was determined to stay alive in order to possess the inheritance promised him by God.

No matter what your age is today, you need to be as determined to possess what God has for you as Caleb was to obtain his inheritance. It will take boldness to receive everything God has for you, especially if you are older.

However, God is no respecter of persons. If He gave Caleb his Promised Land at eighty-five years of age, then He will give you your Promised Land no matter how old you are.

Some Christians have "retired," and they should be ashamed. There is no such thing as retiring in God. It is all right to retire from a job or occupation, if you can afford it, but there is no reason to retire from working for God.

God is God, and He can give you supernatural wisdom and strength enough to possess everything He has for you. Yes, it will take supernatural wisdom and supernatural strength. But if Caleb could get those from God, so can you.

### Supernatural Strength

If you want supernatural strength and wisdom, you must stop watching those carnal, dead programs on television. Even knowing how to "build muscle" in the natural will not help you in the spiritual realm.

Better get your nose in the Book of books and begin reading about a man named

Caleb, who was bold and walked tall even at what is generally considered a ripe old age.

Obedience and wholly following the Lord will give you supernatural strength and bring blessings raining down on you.

I can just hear Caleb saying, "I have as much strength and vitality now as I had when I was forty. In fact, my strength is still so great that I could go out to war, fight, and come back shouting with the victory!"

He was talking about fighting hand-to-hand with swords and spears, not riding inside tanks and firing machine guns.

Also, look at the handicaps he had to overcome in the beginning. He had many disadvantages:

• He had been a slave to Egyptian bondage for forty years, working at hard labor on the equivalent of a chain gang making bricks out of straw.

• He was of a persecuted minority, one which the people of the nation where he lived were prejudiced against.

• He also was of a persecuted minority of two — Joshua and himself — when the other ten spies wanted to run from the Canaanites.

The people were ready to stone Caleb and Joshua, as well as Moses. (Num. 14:10.)

•He wanted to go forward, while millions of his companions wanted to go backward. So he had to suffer for their sakes and mark time in the wilderness until he was an old man.

Perhaps you have had disadvantages in your life.

Perhaps you have had some hard times in different areas of your life.

Perhaps you have had to "mark time" and wait because of other people's mistakes or disobedience.

However, if you will be bold and walk tall in God, you can overcome every disadvantage. You can be like Caleb, the man who was bold enough to ask for a mountain.

# 2
# The Man Who Asked
# for a Mountain

# 2

# The Man Who Asked
# for a Mountain

> **Now therefore give me this mountain, whereof the Lord spake in that day. . . .**
>
> **Joshua 14:12**

Caleb also had courage and determination. He did not ask for something that was easy. He had the boldness to ask for something *big* in God.

Caleb asked for a mountain!

He did not say, "Please, I know I'm getting old, so just give me this little plain down by the riverside. It won't take a lot of work, and I won't have to climb uphill. After all, I've already 'paid my dues' and done my part to help others. We have already taken this little piece of land from the Canaanites."

That is probably what an ordinary person would have asked for, but not Caleb.

No! He said, "Give me something with a little challenge to it. Give me this *mountain*!"

Can you imagine an eighty-five-year-old man asking to be allowed to take in battle and possess an entire mountain?

And this was not just any mountain. This mountain was full of giants. It was fenced and had "great" cities.

> Now therefore give me this mountain, whereof the Lord spake in that day; for thou heardest in that day how the Anakims were there, and that the cities were great and fenced: if so be the Lord will be with me, then I shall be able to drive them out, as the Lord said.
>
> And Joshua blessed him, and gave unto Caleb the son of Jephunneh Hebron for an inheritance.
>
> Joshua 14:12,13

The Anakims were giants, some reportedly as much as ten feet tall. But Joshua granted his request. Therefore, Hebron became the inheritance of Caleb, because he wholly followed the Lord God of Israel. I like that! Personally, from my many visits to the Holy Land, I have found that I like Hebron almost better than any other part of the Holy Land. It is a beautiful area.

Caleb received his inheritance — the land of Hebron — because he determined to walk tall and boldly follow the Lord God of hosts.

You would not believe how many times this phrase, "because he wholly followed the Lord His God," is in the Bible. So many people have obtained their desires from the Lord because of this one thing.

Caleb followed God in complete obedience, which is why he received so much from Him. He drove out the giants, because he was empowered with supernatural strength from walking so close to God.

> **And Caleb drove thence the three sons of Anak, Shesai, and Ahiman, and Talmai, the children of Anak.**
>
> **Joshua 15:14**

What did Caleb think and say was the secret of his success? He never took the glory and credit to himself. He said:

> **...If so be the Lord will be with me, then I shall be able to drive them out, as the Lord said.**
>
> **Joshua 14:12**

Caleb knew that if God was on his side, if God said he could do it, he knew no one could stand against him and succeed.

Because of knowing that, Caleb, at eighty-five, had the supernatural strength, energy, and boldness to ask for a mountain — not a plain and not a valley.

I can just hear him saying to Joshua, "I'll climb that mountain! And, up on that mountaintop, I will fight men twice my size, and I'll 'lick' every one of them. I know I can drive out that bunch, because I'm bold in God!"

Caleb probably took one look at the giants and, like David, said, "I'm coming after you, boys! This is the end of your 'messing around' with the children of Israel."

He won as tremendous a victory as David did years later over Goliath. Caleb drove the giants down to the Mediterranean Sea. That is where they were living, among the Philistines, when David came on the scene. (1 Sam. 17.)

Caleb took their houses away from the giants. Those houses must have had mighty big doors to let in ten-foot giants. Caleb stripped from them everything they had, and Hebron became a holy place. That was where the patriarchs, Abraham, Isaac, and Jacob were buried with their wives.

Notice that the children of Anak were not buried in Hebron in the same area as the patriarchs. The Anakims were not allowed to join that godly crowd, even in death. They did not receive great honor; they did not deserve it.

But Joshua was granted great honor in God. There is even an entire book of the Bible named after him. Caleb also was granted great honor by God. However, there was no honor for the sons of Anak, because those giants came against God's people.

Caleb deserved honor, because he was a generation builder. He established Hebron as his inheritance, and it remains a place many people visit even today. It is a mountain, and it is surrounded by other mountains.

A man, old by our terms, possessed that mountain, because he was bold. He walked tall in God, and he cast a long shadow. His influence was far-reaching. A little mistreated boy, born and reared in poverty, hatred, and slavery became a mighty man of God. No doubt, however, Caleb's greatest celebration of victory was not when he won Hebron, but when he went to heaven.

Young Christians should learn a lesson from men such as Caleb:

• What your parents are or have been does not need to determine what *you* are going to be in God.

• Where you live today does not have to determine where you are going to live.

• What you do today does not have to be what you are going to accomplish for God some day.

• What your parents' life was like does not have to be the pattern for your life. You can be what God *says* you can be!

You do not have to be afraid. If your parents are now poor, that does not mean you always have to be poor. God will help you personally if you just ask Him.

## How To Get Bold in God

There are some fascinating Scriptures that show boldness being produced, such as Acts 4:31, where the followers of Jesus were gathered together praying on the Day of Pentecost. The Bible says that they prayed, the place was shaken, and they **spake the Word of God with boldness.**

Another example of godly boldness is found in Acts 5:15, where Luke reported that multitudes of men and women were added to the Lord. People carried the sick out into the street on beds and couches to lay them where the shadow of the Apostle Peter passing by might fall on them, and they would be healed.

When you are full of the Holy Spirit, even the shadow you cast can be full of power!

This was the same Peter who denied Jesus three times in a matter of hours when Jesus was in hardest trial of His life, a literal trial *for* His life.

This was the same Peter who had "backslid" and gone back to fishing for a living instead of going into the ministry after the crucifixion.

From the time Peter was filled with the Holy Spirit, he became bold. He walked tall in God, and he cast a healing shadow for the world.

God is talking to some Christians today to be bold for Him. He wants us to walk tall in Him. Some Christians hear the Word, and it just goes in one ear and right back out the other. Some Christians *believe* the Word, but the world changers are those who *live* the Word.

What are *you* going to do about being bold in God?

There is a price to pay for greatness, boldness, walking tall in God, and casting a long shadow. I want God to change hearts and change lives, so that the Church as a whole can walk bold in Him and change this world! Those who walk close to God are changed.

Being bold, walking tall, and casting a long shadow has nothing to do with what we call arrogance or pride. For example, when Moses was bold and walked tall in God, the Lord said he was the humblest man on the face of the earth! (Num. 12:3.)

So, if you associate boldness with arrogance, you are missing the point. I am not talking about human arrogance or human boasting: I am talking about being so submerged in God that He can change your life.

God wants to change the world using people like you. However, you will have to move deeper into God for Him to be able to do that. Ask Him for holy boldness. Yes, there is such a thing as holy boldness unto the Lord so that you have something others do not have. You must have the wisdom of God in you, in order for you to be a "life-changer" and a "life-builder" like Caleb.

The entire Church of Jesus Christ needs to become bold in God. They need to walk tall and learn how to cast a long shadow of godly influence on this earth for Jesus.

Do you have a heart like Caleb?

Come up out of "Egypt's" (the world's) sin, degradation, and bondage, and begin to walk with the greatest Man of all time, named Jesus. He will give you boldness. He will give you the ability to walk tall and bold in Him so that you can change the world for His glory.

If you will walk with Jesus wherever He leads you, He will take you into your Promised Land and then on up to heaven. God wants *you*. He will give you supernatural strength, just as He did Caleb. He will make you into one of those who walk bold in the earth to accomplish His purposes.

God does not want us to be "put down" as we live for Him on this earth.

God does not want us to be pushed around as the servants of men. We are to be the mighty servants of the Lord God Almighty. We are to walk tall in the earth. We are to speak the Word of the Almighty, because we are His champions.

Some Christians believe in the Holy Spirit, yet they do not have Him functioning every day in their lives. They need to *move* in the Spirit, *think* in the Spirit, *walk* in the Spirit, and *talk* in the Spirit.

Some Christians think, "But if I get into the operations of the Holy Spirit, there will be problems and disadvantages to me. Even some other Christians will shun me or make fun of me."

Do not let the devil tell you lies like that.

When I was a little boy, other children made fun of me almost every day at school, because my mother belonged to a "full-gospel" church. Their parents belonged to mainline denominations and were highly respected. My mother's little church "made too much noise" out there praising God and "carrying on." So do not talk to me about being embarrassed over the operations of the Spirit! I have been there.

26

Once, I even asked my mother, "Why don't you join another church, so I can have peace at school?"

She said, "Because God wouldn't be happy with us."

I said, "Well, then, let's keep God happy if we can!"

What other people say and do is their business.

What Christians say and do is God's business.

We should make up our minds to walk with God, talk with God, live for God, and be one of His bold ones.

Part-time followers of God will never make it. You must be wholly attached and committed to God. Greatness does not go along with double-mindedness. Greatness goes with a single mind — a mind sold on Jesus.

Be a Caleb — bold and walking tall in God. Walk tall among men. We do not need just *one* Caleb in this earth today. We need a houseful of "Calebs."

We need a multitude of men and women who will say, "I'm bold, and I'm walking tall in God! Therefore, I will never be defeated. The devil does not have any power over me. I am not going to believe the devil's dirty little lies that he tries to speak to me through my mind. I am walking bold in the Word."

We should learn the lessons of the Old Testament in order to profit from the mistakes of those who are examples for us. (1 Cor. 10:11.) The entire Old Testament was not forgotten when the New Testament was written.

It was preserved to teach us how to live in a time like this.

It was preserved for those "upon whom the ends of the world (age) are come." (1 Cor. 10:11.)

### The Bold Learn From the Past

If we do not give much attention to what God has done in the past, He will not be able to do very much in us in the present or in the future.

We need to look at some biblical men of faith to see why they made such an impact upon their worlds. They walked tall in God in their generations and cast a long shadow because their lives influenced other people.

It *is* possible for an ordinary person to become strong in God and walk tall and bold in his generation. Take the Apostle Paul, for example. The Roman emperor Nero thought that after he killed Paul this little Jewish preacher would be forgotten by the world the next day.

However, two thousand years later, we name our sons "Paul" and our dogs "Nero"! It is amazing how the world changes. The once great and powerful Nero is now forgotten, but a lowly servant of God named Paul has been remembered throughout the centuries.

In fact, the Apostle Paul is casting a long shadow even today. He was bold. Although he is said not to have been very large in physical stature, he walked tall in God. He addressed kings and governors and mighty men with great courage and conviction. What a remarkable person he was!

An Old Testament man of faith who walked tall in God and cast a long shadow in his own generation was Moses, Caleb's "mentor" or role model, as we might say today. Caleb had Moses as an example all the way from Egypt to the Promised Land and for the forty-year wilderness trek. No wonder Caleb knew how to be bold and walk tall.

On the other hand, all of the other adult male Israelites had the same example, and they did not become bold. What made the difference? Let's look at the life of Moses and see the thing that made him a man of boldness.

# 3
# The Sheepherder
# Who Became Bold

# 3

# The Sheepherder
# Who Became Bold

God can turn anyone from mediocrity to greatness.

He can change a sheepherder into a mighty leader.

He can turn you from an automobile mechanic to someone great and mighty in Him.

*If* He can get you to turn aside to see what He is doing.

Moses had a divine encounter with God. That is when he became bold and began to walk very tall in God. The great Pharaoh of Egypt shrank to the size of a peanut in this man's presence.

In his generation, this sheepherder named Moses cast a long shadow across the entire nation of Egypt, as well as his own nation of Israel.

Moses was already eighty years old when God cornered him in the Sinai peninsula of the Arabian desert at the base of Mount Horeb. Meeting God was the beginning of Moses' greatness, and when Caleb met God through Moses, he began to become great.

Moses' first meeting with God was out in the desert. While looking after his father-in-law's sheep, Moses came across a sight that would startle anyone — a bush on fire that would not burn up. Possibly the light that radiated out from this burning bush was the same kind of light that guided the wise men from Persia (now Iran) to the Christ child in Bethlehem. It was the *Shekinah* glory of God.

The fire that shone from that bush must have been brilliant, because it attracted Moses' attention to God. When he turned aside to look at it, he had an encounter with God. (Ex. 3:2-10.) Moses took time to turn aside and notice — and he saw what God was doing in the earth. When God saw that Moses had turned aside, He called him by name, and Moses answered, "Here am I."

At that time in his life, Moses must have given up any expectation of becoming great.

His days in the palace of Pharaoh as the adopted, favored son of Pharaoh's daughter were long gone.

He never expected to be remembered for millenniums of time.

He never expected to be remembered down through the ages by millions of people.

Probably, he thought his only destiny was a final trip to the grave, a trip to be buried deep in the sands of the wilderness. But, suddenly, in an instant of time, he "turned aside" and had an encounter with the living God, and everything changed.

From that one confrontation, we find a man totally changed by the power of God! Moses became bold. He talked bold, walked bold, and stood tall in the knowledge of God. He was not afraid of anyone any longer. That is how he came to cast a long shadow over two nations — Egypt and Israel — in his own lifetime, and many nations since.

When I traveled through the Sinai desert at various times, I have been shown an interesting little tree that looks something like an umbrella. It is called "a Moses tree."

Natives say that is the kind of tree which has always been in the desert. They say this might have been the kind of bush that attracted Moses' attention as it burned brightly with the fire of God.

God performs wonders for many people who do not even bother to turn aside to notice what is going on. They pay no attention to what God is doing in the earth. Many people are so busy with this world's affairs that, when they hit eternity and go to hell, they will not even know what happened until it is too late!

Someone told me recently about the owner of a company for which he had worked. The man owns mansions in about eight different nations and spends his time flying from one to another in his own private plane. A multimillionaire, he does business from exotic places.

However, he has one big problem: He is afraid to die.

It is foolish to be afraid to die. It is inevitable, and if something is inevitable, there is no use being afraid of it. You had better just get acquainted with it.

**Get Acquainted With the Inevitable**

In the ancient courts of the world, there once was a court jester (sometimes called "a court fool"). These men were in the business of being funny in front of kings. It was their profession to tell jokes, do juggling acts, or whatever it took to keep the king in a good mood. They worked hard to take the minds of kings off their troubles. If they did not succeed, it might be "off" with their heads!

One day, the king said to this court jester, "If you ever find a person crazier than you are, would you give him my royal scepter?" And the king handed his scepter to the jester.

The court jester answered, "Your Majesty, I've already found one."

"Well, who is it?" the king asked.

"It's you," the jester replied, as he handed the king back his symbol of authority.

"Why do you think I am crazier than you?" the king asked.

The jester replied, "I have one question to ask you. Your answer will determine whether you are crazier than I. At this very moment, you are on a journey through life.

But are you acquainted with the King on the other side of the river of death?"

Dumbfounded, the king answered, "No!"

And the jester replied, "Then you are the biggest fool I have ever met. You are a king enjoying vast wealth, but if you have not made preparation to meet the King on the other side of the river, you are in bad shape."

There is much truth in that story. Millions have descended into hell from all of the nations and times of the earth because they did not take time to turn aside and see what God was doing in the earth. So they never became acquainted with Him.

Turn aside unto God! Do not be afraid of death. You can get acquainted with the One who has the power over death. One encounter with God can change your life forever. He wants you to turn aside and fellowship with Him. He wants you to see His glory.

When you spend time with your heavenly Father, you will walk tall and mighty in Him. That is what happened to Moses. He met God, and it changed his destiny.

Moses said, "God, I will accept your challenge. I will take on your commission."

At first, Moses was like most of us. He was afraid to do what God called him to do. He was afraid that he was not capable enough, smart enough, talented enough, and could not speak well enough. Most of us have felt, or feel, the same way. But we need to remember that it is God who does the equipping and the empowering.

Finally, Moses agreed and returned to Egypt to fulfill God's commission and deliver his own people from bondage. However, he did not return the way he had left, fleeing from justice after having killed a man. After his encounter with God, he stood as a new man. Something had happened to him.

That one encounter changed Moses from a desert shepherd to a mighty giant in the Lord. God wants to change you in the same way. But an encounter with the living God will only occur when you take time to turn aside and see what God is doing. Enquire of Him and see what He wants to do through you. See what He wants to say through you, then the fire of God will burn in your heart and never go out. You will be changed into a different person.

When Moses arrived in Egypt, it looked as if he had failed almost before he got started. However, by the time he led the Israelites out of Egypt, things had changed. Moses was bold and walked tall. His people left Egypt heavily laden with treasure.

There is something about walking tall in God and casting a long shadow that will change people and nations for God's glory. Your boldness influences others. Other people will be drawn to you, and you can help them change their destinies and walk tall in God also.

### Bold People Affect Others

As soon as Moses appeared on the horizon of time, walking boldly and casting a long shadow, the man named Caleb attached himself to Moses and did not leave him until the day Moses went to heaven.

I believe Caleb looked at Moses and thought, "He is bold in God, and he casts a long shadow. His influence is going to be felt around the world. I want to follow him." So Caleb wrapped his destiny around Moses.

Most of us need the influence of bold people in our lives. We get weak when we are with weak people, but we learn to be bold when we make bold people our role models.

God preserved this account of Caleb in the Bible for our admonition. Therefore, we need to know what made him great. Caleb was:

• An Israelite of the seed of Abraham.

• Destined, before Moses came, to live and die a mere slave because his parents were slaves before him.

• Born with his life in danger from a Pharaoh who murdered the male Israelite babies as a form of population control.

Caleb was born into the earth at a very sad and dangerous time for him. He and his forebears, descendants of Jacob, grandson of Abraham, had been in Egypt more than four hundred years. At first, they had favor with Pharaoh, because Joseph, son of Jacob, was prime minister.

However, as the years passed and rulers gained the throne who did not remember Joseph, the fortunes of the Israelites declined. America is only a little more than

39

two hundred years old as a nation, which gives us little perspective on how a Pharaoh could arise in four hundred years who did not know Joseph. Time obscures even the greatest of rulers.

Caleb had an advantage over some of the other slave children. He had a godly mother. Godly mothers are sweet and full of character. She must have been an interesting woman, because Caleb's greatness began with her. She had the courage to name her son — born a slave and the son of slaves — a challenging name. Some mothers do great things for God.

She named her son "Bold." That is what Caleb means, according to *Dake's Annotated Bible*. Everytime someone spoke to him, they called him, "Bold!" Everytime he was called for a meal, he was reminded that he was "Bold."

From birth, every time people addressed him, they really were saying, "Bold, what are you doing? Bold, where are you going? Bold, what are you going to do next?"

The Israelites began to know him as "the bold one." In the natural, Caleb had no advantages to go along with his name. Then what made him different from other men?

As a slave, he was not any different from other slaves. In fact, we do not really see any difference in Caleb until he was forty years old.

Then a certain man came into his life. God sends men to us who change and influence our lives. Moses influenced many people for God. Your life could be changed some day because of someone else's godly influence. And you could change someone else's life, if you walk tall and act bold in the Lord.

For the first time in his life, Caleb saw a man of his own race who walked bold in God. When Moses came walking into sophisticated Egypt from the "backside" of the desert, he declared, "I've heard from God!"

That statement will get your attention in a hurry!

He told the Israelites that God had sent him to set them free.

He told the Israelites that they must be bold and walk tall in the Lord their God.

Because of Moses' influence, Caleb also became bold. Personally, I do not believe Moses was ever out of Caleb's sight for any length of time. At first, Moses may not have noticed him very much, but it could not have been long before Caleb caught the attention of the leader of Israel.

Study Caleb's life and you will see that he was on the right side every time a decision was made, whether it was in the desert or anywhere else. He always was on the right side, which was God's side. He never opposed Moses, so he never opposed God.

In all of the transgressions of Israel during that forty-year journey, Caleb is never mentioned. He stood against every rebellion ever attempted against Moses. He stuck with Moses all the way. He was a true friend and a true follower.

Caleb probably was right there when the death angel walked through Egypt.

Caleb was probably right there when Moses raised his rod and told the Red Sea to back off and stand up in a heap. (Ex. 15.) More than likely, he was one of the first to race across the dry river bed to safety on the other shore.

Caleb saw Moses work the works of God. I am sure he got bigger on the inside every time he saw Moses pronounce the judgments of God and the laws of God.

When Moses asked Caleb to be one of the twelve representatives of the tribes of Israel to search the land of Canaan, that may have been the greatest thing he ever asked him to do. The Bible says that each of these men was a ruler in his own tribe. (Num. 13:2,3.)

During that walk from Egypt, apparently Caleb had gained some prestige among the people. He was a leader among his people already. Out of the twelve, only two saw victory. The other ten saw giants.

If you are bold and walking tall in God, you also are only going to see victory. If you are bold, you are taller than any giant. You can cast down giants in the name of Jesus, no matter what kind of giants they are. You never have to go down in defeat.

Those who are bold in God do not know defeat. They only know victory. The war is not over until it is over, and we are going to win the war.

Caleb and Joshua saw the same giants as the other ten. They saw the same walled cities and the same huge gates. However, they saw something that the other spies did not. They saw God.

When they returned, Caleb gave a great report, a report full of faith, filled with boldness and courage. Big walls and big men could not stop Caleb from walking tall in God. I am not talking about his physical stature. The kind of walking tall that I mean occurs in faith and on the inside.

Caleb not only gave a good report, but he said, "Let's go up at once and take this land." (Num. 14:6-8.) *At once* means "right now." No hesitating, wavering, or doubting. He even said, "They are bread for us!"

He was going to eat "gianties" for breakfast, not "Wheaties®." You know that you are bold and walking tall in God when you can make your boast in Him. Boldness in God casts a long shadow of faith and godly influence over people.

### Boldness Is Following Jesus

What is boldness? It simply is following Jesus. It is being obedient. When you are bold in Jesus, you can just knock your enemies out of your way. You do not follow man. You do not get discouraged.

Caleb tried to tell the other Israelites how to walk tall in God, but they would not listen to him. They even hated him for being so bold. He may have had to wait forty years, but he won and they lost. Their bodies were buried beneath the sand, as God had said, and he went on to possess a mountain and judge Israel. (Num. 14:29,30.)

I feel sorry for Caleb, having to watch his friends and relatives — all the Israelites over twenty years of age — die of doubt and unbelief in the desert and be buried in the sand. Perhaps he had to assist with many of their burials. He may have seen as many as two million people die because of dis-obedience.

However, he could claim that, of the times Israel rebelled during the forty-two times they moved from place to place during that forty years, he was never one who grumbled. He was never bitten by a snake. He was always one of those standing by Moses and supporting him.

The result is that one day Caleb walked in Moses' shoes as one of the leaders of Israel. Caleb was not only the first man to go into the Promised Land, but he was the last man to lead the Israelites before the judges and prophets began to rule.

Disobedience cost the Israelites their promised inheritance and, eventually, their lives. It even cost Moses, Aaron, and their sister, Miriam.

Moses lived until the very last day before the Israelites were permitted to enter the land of Canaan.

Then God cut him off saying, "You can't go in to possess the land, because when I asked you to speak to the rock, you hit it with a stick instead, saying, '*Must we . . . Shall God and I?*' . . . " (Num. 20:10.)

No matter how bold you get or how tall you walk in God, He does not need you to take the credit with Him.

A lot of people make Moses' mistake when they say, "God and I are going to do thus-and-so in the earth."

No, it is God who is going to do something mighty in the earth: We are just to pronounce what He does.

We are just to say, "In the name of Jehovah, let it be done!"

Presumption, or tempting God, is one of the five sins that will hinder you from success in the Lord. Christians should be very aware of the five sins that brought disaster on an entire adult generation of Israel.

The Church of Jesus Christ will never be able to walk tall and cast a long shadow of influence in this world, if we allow these sins in our lives.

# 4
# Five Sins That Will Hinder Boldness

# 4

# Five Sins That Will Hinder Boldness

**But with many of them God was not well pleased: for they were overthrown in the wilderness.**
**1 Corinthians 10:5**

The five sins which Israel committed in the wilderness are listed in 1 Corinthians 10:6-10. These are sins that will destroy any civilization. However, there is no record in the Bible that Caleb or Joshua were involved in any of these sins.

Paul wrote that all of the "fathers" traveled under the cloud of God, and all passed through the Red Sea. He said:

• All were baptized unto Moses in the cloud and in the sea.

• All ate the same spiritual meat and drank the same spiritual drink.

• All drank of Christ, the Rock who followed them.

But, Paul wrote, God was not pleased with many of them.

Why was that? God was displeased because of these five sins that Paul went on to describe.

Now these things were our examples, to the intent that *we should not lust* after evil things, as they also lusted.

*Neither be* ye *idolators,* as were some of them; as it is written, The people sat down to eat and drink, and rose up to play.

*Neither let us commit fornication,* as some of them committed, and fell in one day three and twenty thousand.

*Neither let us tempt Christ,* as some of them also tempted, and were destroyed of serpents.

*Neither murmur* ye, as some of them also murmured, and were destroyed of the destroyer.

**1 Corinthians 10:6-10**

The number-one sin committed by the Israelites was *lust.*

They were always clamoring, "Give us meat! Give us this! Give us that!"

They never were satisfied with God. They could not seem to remember that He was the one who brought them out of bondage where their hands were blistered from rough work and their backs bent from hard labor.

They lusted after food, sex, and even over being endued with the same power Moses had. They were full of lust.

Just a few days after leaving Egypt and seeing the great love and protection of God for them, they fell back into idolatry. When Moses was on the mountain receiving the Ten Commandments longer than they thought he ought to be, they pressured Aaron to make them a golden calf to worship.

They offered sacrifices to this calf, one of the gods of Egypt, had a great feast, and then began to participate in an orgy. They not only were lustful and idolatrous, but they also committed adultery and fornication as part of the worship of the calf.

The judgment of God killed twenty-three thousand of them when Moses came down the mountain and found out what they had been doing.

Later, they tempted God and many were bitten by snakes.

The desert was full of snakes, and God had protected them up to this point. All He had to do was remove His strength and protective power from the Israelites for them to be bitten. Suddenly, they were dying all over the place from snake bites.

Moses made a brazen serpent on God's instructions and held it up for the people to look upon (a type of the cross of Christ), or they all would have died. (Num. 21:9.)

There are many ways to tempt God. One of those is blaming Him.

Some Christians actually have the presumption to blame God!

They say, "God, You didn't do this! You didn't do that! Why did You let this happen? Why did that happen?"

We are too small to be blaming the God of the universe for anything. Many things happen for which we do not have the answers. I know that God is a good God, and what He does is always right. For anyone to stand up and accuse God of anything is foolishness.

Some people blame God for things that happened to them as children.

They will say things such as, "Something bad happened to me when I was eight years old. I'm not going to serve God."

My, how foolish that is.

I have lived my entire life on the premise that God knows best, that He is always right. I am ready to be taken home, or I am ready to remain on earth. I am ready to do anything God wants me to do, and I am not going to quarrel with Him about it. I will not find fault with Him no matter what happens.

The last sin Paul mentioned of the Israelites was that they "murmured," and boy, did they murmur!

It is so easy to murmur, to grumble and complain. It is so easy to find fault with the Church. However, no one is perfect. Let us keep our personal feelings washed by the blood of Jesus Christ and keep the important things in mind.

The important thing is to get people saved. We are soldiers in the army of God. We are supposed to go out and fight the devil. We are to take souls from him that he has stolen.

If you ever lose the vision for souls, you will not know what you are doing.

People who say, "What am I doing with my life? What am I supposed to be doing?" are not winning a lot of souls to Jesus.

Perhaps you say, "But I don't know how to win souls."

I can tell you how in two minutes:

Get your hands full of tracts, go from house to house, give people a tract, and ask if they are born again. Then, pray with them. You would be amazed how many each Christian could win to Jesus that way.

Perhaps you think you are too timid. But you are not timid out at the ball game cheering and shouting for *your* team. Why should you get timid witnessing for Jesus? And why should you be timid in church?

These five sins that Israel committed will keep anyone from walking bold and tall in God and from casting a long shadow of influence in the world.

These five sins will keep you timid, sidetracked, and wondering what to do with your life.

If you want to win souls, avoid these five sins, and walk bold. Boldness attracts other people to God.

# 5
# Boldness Influences
# People for God

# 5

# Boldness Influences People for God

**Forty years old was I when Moses the servant of the Lord sent me from Kadesh Barnea to spy out the land, and I brought him word again,** *as it was in mine heart.*

**Joshua 14:7**

By the time Moses was ready to change his address from this world to the next, his influence on Caleb had become obvious. Caleb was a winner, not a loser. In fact, from the time he was set free from Egyptian bondage, Caleb only had a history of winning and winning and winning.

After forty years of wandering in the wilderness, and after more than a million people had died from rebellion and disobedience, Joshua and Caleb finally walked into the Promised Land.

Caleb was remembering the time forty years before when he brought Moses word about the land. He was remembering vividly, I am sure, when they first arrived, and he was sent with Joshua and the other ten to spy on the Canaanites.

Notice that he says, "I brought Moses the news of Canaan *as it was in my heart*."

When Caleb spied out the land, he came back and told the Israelites what was in his *heart*, not what was in his *head*.

His head might have said what the other ten spies said, "This is impossible! The walls are tall, and so are the giants. How are we going to do this?"

However, Caleb was of another spirit (Num. 14:24), another attitude, and he walked tall in his faith in God. He returned from the spy trip and gave Moses a report based on what was in his heart.

You see, the wrong witness and the wrong testimony can discourage people.

Sometimes you hear Christians say, "I tell you, I've had a hard time in life! I don't know anything but hard times."

Why don't they pray it through? If I have a problem, I pray through on it. That way, I do not know hard times when I meet them on the road. I have prayed it out.

For example, all over the world, I have had to accomplish the impossible. I have had to establish churches by faith. We built a church in Manila by faith. There were a few friends in America who gave to that project, but actually, our friends seemed to get fewer the whole time we were building that church!

Then God healed a little girl, and the whole country was set on fire. A six-week revival began in the park. I took my station wagon every night with a big trunk in it, and every night, people giving in the offering filled it up with money.

God built that building. When the revival was going on, we never told anyone how much it would cost to build that church. We had not paid the contractor yet, but he trusted us. When that revival broke out, he needed money to be able to continue with construction. So we would pay him with bags of money. He would walk out with two men helping him carry the bags.

In other words, that revival paid for the church building.

Do you know that it takes revival to pay for things for God? Are you wondering why this is? It is because "dead" people do not give. They have spiritual arthritis and cannot even get their hands in their pocket to give.

When there is a revival, you can build a skyscraper. That is because, when the joy of the Lord is present, people want to give so much, they do not know what to do. That church in the Philippines is a miracle church. Today, it is valued at six to eight million American dollars.

That is what God can do. If He has never done that for you, ask yourself if you have opened your heart to give to Him? I give to God almost every day of my life. Even if I give to the wrong people, I would rather be a "sucker" occasionally than to give no one anything.

Being bold and walking tall does not mean you will not encounter problems in life. You will, and you will sometimes have to do the impossible in God. But, when you "pray through," you will see God solve the problems.

So Caleb was able to give Moses and the people a good report, because he told them what was in his heart, not his head.

However, he said the "brethren" who went into the land with him "made the heart of the people to melt." (Josh. 14:8.) Caleb meant their hearts melted with fear.

## How Do You Influence People?

Let me ask you this question: What influence do you have on other people?

Do you make people sad by the way you live?

Do you make their hearts melt with fear, doubt, and unbelief?

Or do you inspire them to have faith in God?

The other spies reduced the people's faith so that they could not walk bold in God as they were supposed to walk. Those ten men came back with the wrong interpretation of what God was able to do.

They apparently thought possessing the land with giants in it was *too hard* for God!

They forgot that He had killed the firstborn of all Egypt and spared them.

They forgot that He had parted the Red Sea, drowned Pharaoh with his soldiers and chariots, and allowed them to cross on dry ground.

They forgot the thunderings from the top of Mount Sinai and the Ten Commandments written in stone by the finger of God.

How could they forget all these things?

They forgot God's past miracles for one simple reason: They focused on the negative and could not see the greatness of God.

The result of allowing fear to be instilled in their hearts was that the Israelites could not follow the Lord *wholly*. That is an old English word that means *entirely*.

Caleb followed God and did not sin, because he *wholly* followed God. His heart was toward God, and he made decisions out of his heart not his head.

That is why God promised him that he would enter the Promised Land when all the other men over twenty, except Joshua, were not allowed to see it.

Walking tall in God means to serve Him *wholly*, and that means to walk in absolute obedience, not eighty or ninety percent obedience. *Wholly* following the Lord does not mean withholding the tithe and trying to get God to bless you when you have not done what you are supposed to do. (Mal. 3:10.)

Entering in to all that God promised you is the reward of the bold. It is the reward of those who walk tall in God. It is for *you*, if you will enter in to it.

Caleb was not like the average Israelite. He was nothing like them at all, as we have seen. He was born in slavery just as they had been. He had experienced the same things they had. He was of the same lineage as they. Yet he was different.

The reason, according to the Bible, is that he was "of a different spirit." What was that "spirit"? It was the spirit, or attitude, of faith.

Ask God to create a super-duper spirit in you. He can give you a good spirit, a sweet spirit, so that you go around hugging everyone and smiling.

You feel like shaking hands with everyone and saying, "God bless you!"

With an attitude like that, you will refresh many people.

If you have an excellent spirit in you, you will not run away from church as soon as the service is over. Church is to be a place of fellowship. Christians are a family, a family in God, and we need each member of the family to flow together.

If you want to gain your inheritance from God, then you must walk tall and act bold in His service. To move in that boldness, you must be of a different spirit than many others. Boldness will not be true boldness without faith.

You might say that boldness is the expression of faith and trust in God. Boldness is confidence that God is good, that He is always right, and that He is in charge. Boldness never doubts, never disobeys, and never is afraid.

Be a Caleb and begin to take your mountain for God!

**Dr. Lester Sumrall** is founder and chairman of a worldwide missionary outreach, LeSEA Inc. Respected throughout the world as a missionary statesman, Dr. Sumrall has raised up churches and  taught the Word of God for more than sixty years. In addition, he maintains headquarters for LeSEA Global and LeSEA Broadcasting (international radio and television) in South Bend, Indiana, where he pastors Christian Center Cathedral of Praise. His three married sons, Frank, Stephen, and Peter also are involved in the ministry.

Dr. Sumrall, a prolific author, has written more than 110 books and teaching syllabi. In addition to his writing, he is founder and president of Indiana Christian University and is host on the television programs, "World Harvest" and "The Lester Sumrall Teaching Series."

A powerful and dynamic speaker, Dr. Sumrall ministers God's message with authority and takes advantage of electronic media to reach the world today. He founded LeSEA Broadcasting, Inc., which owns and operates eleven television stations in the following cities:

WHMB TV-40 Indianapolis, Indiana

WHME TV-46 South Bend, Indiana

KWHB TV-47 Tulsa, Oklahoma

KWHE TV-14 Honolulu, Hawaii

WHKE TV-55 Kenosha, Wisconsin

KWHD TV-53 Denver, Colorado

KWHH TV-14 Hilo, Hawaii

KWHM TV-21 Maui, Hawaii

WHNO TV-20 New Orleans, Louisiana

W15AM Grand Rapids, Michigan

K69EK Oklahoma City, Oklahoma

A recent outreach to the world's hungry has thrust Dr. Sumrall into a new dimension of showing compassion to the far corners of the earth in response to our Lord's command to "feed the hungry." Called the *End Time Joseph Program To Feed the Hungry*, Dr. Sumrall is enlisting worldwide pastor-to-pastor support of this program. It is his belief that government alone should not shoulder the responsibility of caring for the world's homeless, hungry, and needy, but that the Church is to be a responsible vehicle of Christ to suffering humanity.

To receive Lester Sumrall's monthly magazine, *World Harvest*, write:

Lester Sumrall
P.O. Box 12
South Bend, Indiana 46624

*Please include your prayer requests
and comments when you write.*

For information
about Lester Sumrall's
Indiana Christian University, write
for a free catalog about ICU
or about correspondence studies:

Indiana Christian University
P.O. Box 12
South Bend, Indiana 46624

## Other Books by Lester Sumrall

*Pioneers of Faith*
*The Militant Church*
*Overcoming Compulsive Desires*
*101 Questions and Answers on Demon Powers*

*How To Cope Series:*
*Depression*
*Loneliness*
*Rejection*
*Worry*
*Suicide*
*Living Free*

*Miracles Don't Just Happen*
*Demons: The Answer Book*
*Run With the Vision*
*Ecstasy*
*The Face of Jesus*
*Bitten by Devils*
*Life Story*
*Courage to Conquer*

**Available from your local bookstore.**

**Harrison House**

**Tulsa, Oklahoma 74153**

In Canada, contact: Word Alive, P.O. Box 670
Niverville, Manitoba  CANADA R0A 1E0